DEATH *in* Godshill

AN ISLE OF WIGHT TRAGEDY

PETER JAMES CAVE

DEATH *in* Godshill

AN ISLE OF WIGHT TRAGEDY

MEMOIRS

Cirencester

Published by Memoirs

MEMOIRS
PUBLISHING

25 Market Place, Cirencester, Gloucestershire, GL7 2NX
info@memoirsbooks.co.uk www.memoirspublishing.com

First published in England, December 2012

Book jacket design Ray Lipscombe

ISBN 978-1-909544-05-5

Printed in England

CONTENTS

∽

Acknowledgements

Introduction

About the author

ACKNOWLEDGEMENTS

The National Archives

Isle of Wight Register Office

Hampshire County Council Records Office

The Hampshire Chronicle

The Isle of Wight County Press

The Isle of Wight Records Office

The Isle of Wight History Centre

Air war over the Island by H J T Leal, published by
The Isle of Wight County Press

A Lance for Liberty by J D Casswell QC, published
by George Harrap & Co Ltd

Bernard Spilsbury – his life and cases by Browne and Tullett,
published by George Harrap & Co Ltd

Portrait of Sir Bernard Spilsbury by Elliott & Fry

Lethal Witness by Andrew Rose QC, published by
Sutton Publishing Ltd

The Spy Beside the Sea by Adrian Searle,
published by The History Press

*This book is dedicated to my dear wife,
Vicki, without her consistent
enthusiasm and encouragement this would
not have been possible.*

INTRODUCTION

In October 1940 the peaceful, rural setting of East Appleford Farm, near Godshill on the Isle of Wight, was the scene of the shooting of a 61-year-old farmer called Frank Cave. His 25-year-old housekeeper, Mabel Attrill, was charged with his murder.

Sir Bernard Spilsbury, Home Office Pathologist, conducted the post mortem and gave evidence for the Crown. The notorious case of Dr Crippen and his apprehension by the newly-invented telegraph system in 1910 had elevated Sir Bernard to celebrity status. He went on to give evidence for the prosecution in nearly 200 murder trials, including numerous highly-publicised cases such as the 'Brides in the Bath' and the 'Brighton Trunk Murders'. Only a few of the cases ended in an acquittal for the accused.

Mabel Attrill was remanded in custody by the Isle of Wight Magistrates and committed for trial at Winchester Assizes. By an odd twist of fate, she was not the only woman from the Isle of Wight awaiting trial at the Assizes. The case preceding hers was that of Dorothy O'Grady from Sandown, the only woman during World War Two to be charged as a spy. She was found guilty and sentenced to death.

Joshua Casswell led Mabel's defence. In 1935 he had pursued an appeal in the House of Lords, which was probably the most important case on evidence in English criminal law, namely *Woolmington v Director of Public Prosecutions 1935*. The facts of this case bore a resemblance to what happened at East Appleford nearly six years later. The consequences for English law were irrevocable, and the case had a profound effect upon the result in Mabel's trial.

Casswell went on to a distinguished career as a defence barrister. By the time of his retirement in 1951 he had defended around forty people on charges of murder, saving all but five of them from the gallows. Perhaps his most high profile case was in 1946, when he unsuccessfully defended the sadistic murderer Neville Heath.

ABOUT THE AUTHOR

Peter Cave was born on the Isle of Wight and brought up in the village of Chale. His grandparents ran a pub at nearby Blackgang. He left the Island in 1968 having qualified as a Trading Standards Officer, and spent most of his working life enforcing consumer protection law. He has a law degree from London University and is a Member of The Chartered Institute of Arbitrators.

Frank Cave was his great uncle.

CHAPTER ONE

A FARMER AND HIS HOUSEKEEPER

⌒

Until the 1970s it would not have been apparent to any visitor to the Isle of Wight, nor indeed to many locals, that East Appleford Farm was in the parish of Godshill. A local government re-organisation at that time created the new parish of Rookley, and at least for administrative purposes that is where the former farmhouse has since stood.

The building is on a narrow country road, which runs due south from the small village of Rookley to the villages of Chale and Niton, on the coast some six miles away. Rookley was once famous for its production of bricks, but the brickyard closed in 1974. The farm is about two miles from the village of Godshill as the crow flies, but is separated by a wild and barren area of high ground known as Bleakdown, which forms a natural divide from the quintessential English village. Gravel extraction had begun on the down in the 1920s, but the site of the gravel works had subsequently been used as a landfill site for the local council.

The village of Godshill, with its thatched cottages and old-world charm, has become a tourist attraction. Its shops offer local crafts and produce and a model village depicts the area in miniature. A former blacksmith's, known as the Old Smithy, is now a gift shop and tearoom. Overlooking the village is All Saints Church, dating from the 15th century and among the top 10 most visited churches in the UK, apparently attracting more than 100,000 visitors a year. According to legend, local people tried to build the church lower down in the village, where the Griffin Hotel now stands, but overnight the stones were mysteriously moved to the top of the hill. After this had happened three times the locals concluded that the hilltop must be God's chosen site, so they built the church there and the village became known as Godshill.

East Appleford Farm stands a world away from the tourism of the village. It is a four-bedroomed brick Edwardian building with a row of farm cottages across the road from the farm entrance. Its nearest neighbour, about half a mile further down the road, is the Chequers Inn. Very little has changed to either the farmhouse or the locality since the events of October 1940.

At that time the farm was run by Frank Cave. Frank was born in 1880 and in his early years lived with his mother and father at No 10 Trafalgar Road, Newport, together with his sister Rose, four years his junior, and his two younger brothers, Edward and William.

In 1899 Frank married Beatrice Bradley, who like him was 19 years old. They moved to No 7 Trafalgar Road and in due course produced nine children. Frank ran his own small business as a carrier and general contractor. Along with his two younger brothers, he survived the Great War, but the days of the horse-drawn carrier business were in decline. He also needed more accommodation for his large and growing family, so he started a new career as a farmer at East Appleford.

Frank's younger brother Edward had for some time run a small one-man business delivering coal. With his youngest brother William, who was demobilised in 1919, he formed a partnership that traded under the name Cave Brothers, delivering horse-drawn coal and wood. They ran it successfully for the next ten years, serving many of Frank's former customers.

By the early 1930s, the marriage of Frank and Beatrice was on a downward spiral. In 1934 Beatrice moved out of the farmhouse and went to live with their married daughter, Doris Whittington, at No 4 Appleford Cottages, just across the road from the farm. Within a year Frank had taken on a housekeeper – Mabel Attrill.

Mabel Attrill was born Mabel Victoria Kingswell in June 1915 at Pound Farm, Sandford, just to the east of the village of Godshill. Mabel's mother was housekeeper at the farm, which had existed since late Georgian times. Until 1994 it was a working farm, but it has since been converted to holiday accommodation.

In 1931, when Mabel was 16, her mother married Frank Attrill, a widower living in Wootton, and from then on Mabel was known as Mabel Attrill. Just over three years later she moved into East Appleford Farm as the housekeeper to Frank Cave, thirty-five years her senior.

Mabel was around four feet eleven inches tall and of slim build. When she was about twelve years of age she contracted tuberculosis, which affected her left hip. She was treated at home and at various hospitals. The disease left her with one leg shorter than the other. Because of this illness her attendance at school between the ages of 12 and 14 was very irregular.

In the spring of 1940 Beatrice had attempted a reconciliation with Frank and had moved back into the farmhouse. However this had lasted no more than a few weeks, as she found it to be intolerable to live in the house with another woman, so she walked out and returned to live with her daughter across the road.

By the autumn, with the war starting its second year, enemy aircraft action was increasing. Although the Island did not suffer air raids on the scale of some mainland towns and cities, it suffered considerable loss of life and damage to property. During the course of the war more than 800 casualties were recorded on the Island and nearly 11,000 buildings were damaged or destroyed. Life and work at the farm had to continue as best they could.

On the 26th September a Messerschmitt 110, a heavy fighter/bomber, crash-landed on Bleakdown. This type of plane had proved valuable to the Luftwaffe in the Polish campaign, but not so in the Battle of Britain, when it came up against single-engined fighters and its vulnerability was shown. Whereas the Messerschmitt 109 was a match for the Spitfires and Hurricanes, the 110 was not. It lacked the manoeuvrability of the two main RAF fighters and presented a bigger target as well. With only one rear-firing machine gun, it proved an easier target for a Spitfire or Hurricane attacking from the rear. This was what had happened to this particular unlucky 110. Returning from a bombing raid on Southampton, it was picked out from behind by a Hurricane, and although the pilot attempted evasive action he could not throw off his pursuer. The pilot and gunner survived the crash landing but were quickly taken prisoner by soldiers of the Black Watch who were billeted in a house in Rookley.

CHAPTER TWO

THE SHOOTING

Fifteen-year-old Herbert Smith, who was employed by Frank Cave as a farmhand, arrived at East Appleford Farm around 6.30 on the morning of Sunday 20th October 1940, as he did most days. Herbert lived with his mother and father at Dolecoft Dairy in Rookley, about a mile's walk away. The first thing he did each morning was to bring the cows in from the fields for milking. The cowshed stood some 15 yards away from the farmhouse.

Herbert started milking around 7.15 am. About a quarter of an hour later he heard what he thought to be a gunshot, but thinking that someone must be rabbiting, it did not particularly disturb him, so he continued with the milking. Herbert finished the milking around eight o'clock and then took some of the milk in a large can into the dairy. The dairy was attached to the rear of the farmhouse, with its entrance through the porch at the side of the house. As Herbert went through the porch he saw a double-barrelled shotgun standing on its butt in the corner.

He took the cows back to the field and came back to the cowshed about fifteen minutes later. He then saw Mabel Attrill and Doris Whittington talking near the back door.

Earlier that morning, Doris was in bed in her cottage across the road when she heard a tap at the door. It was about 7.40 am. She went downstairs and opened the front door to be confronted by Mabel, who simply said 'Come quick, the old man is shot!'

Doris grabbed her slippers, pulled on her coat and ran after Mabel to the farmhouse. She ran through the back door straight into the scullery, where she saw her father lying on the floor in a pool of blood. He was flat on his back with his arms at his side, his feet nearest the sink and his head forwards the kitchen door. As she lifted her father's head in her arms he took his last breath, but not a word came from Frank's lips. Doris dutifully closed his eyes and mouth and carefully placed a nearby cushion under his head.

Unusually for those times and the farm's location, it was connected to the telephone. Doris ran into the hall and called the local doctor, quickly followed by a call to the police station at Godshill. While she was waiting for the doctor Doris looked at Mabel, who appeared to be dazed, as if she was in a trance. Her hair and clothing looked normal, and she was still carrying on her usual household duties.

Doris noticed that Mabel had a red eye, as if she had recently received a blow. She also saw what appeared to be blood on her thumb.

As Doris had come through the porch she had noticed a shotgun in the corner, one that looked like her father's gun. She knew he usually kept it in the kitchen in the corner near the dresser, and was always particular about the gun being left unloaded.

Within a short time the doctor, Dr Arthur Arbuthnot Stratton, arrived. On receiving Doris' phone call he had driven from his home at Bradley Lodge in Medina Avenue, Newport, to arrive at East Appleford just before quarter past eight. There in the scullery he saw the body of Frank Cave.

Dr Stratton examined the body and found an injury in the left loin, which he assumed was a gunshot wound. He noticed that a fair amount of blood had soaked into the clothing. He then carefully moved the body on its right side, when he could see a large wound. There was no sign of a wound at the front of the body.

The body was fully dressed and still warm, with no signs of rigor mortis having set in. Dr Stratton estimated that the deceased had been dead about half to three quarters of an hour. He could see no indication of any struggle having taken place in the scullery.

During this time he had noticed Mabel coming in and out of the scullery. He asked her how the shooting had happened, to which she replied that they had been quarrelling. She went on to tell him that Frank had threatened her with a gun. She said it had happened near the fireplace and that he had taken a few steps towards the sink and collapsed.

Dr Stratton returned to his home and made a report to the local police.

After the doctor had left, Doris asked Mabel how it had happened. She replied that they had been struggling, the gun had gone off and it was 'either him or me'. She went on to say that it was all over 'a party coming rabbiting'. Doris knew that when she mentioned the word 'party' she was referring to a

Mrs Ellen Evans, an acquaintance of Frank's who often went rabbiting on his land with her brothers. Mabel continued to say that Frank had loaded the gun and had meant it for her.

Later that morning Doris saw Mrs Evans in her car parked outside the farm entrance.

★ ★ ★ ★ ★

Police Constable Stanley Sampson was stationed at the Police House in Chale. This was not a police station in the modern sense but a detached three-bedroomed house in the road leading to the Terrace, opposite the village Post Office at the bottom of Blyth Shute. Around eight o'clock on that Sunday morning PC Sampson had received a telephone call from his headquarters to report the incident at East Appleford Farm. Finishing his breakfast, pulling on his uniform and attaching his bicycle clips, he arrived at the farm about ten past nine. There he saw Doris, who quickly explained what had happened.

PC Sampson could see the body of a man lying on the scullery floor and knew it to be Frank Cave. He stepped back into the porch and saw a twelve-bore shotgun. He picked up the gun, examined it and found the right-hand hammer down and an empty cartridge case in the right barrel. The left hand barrel did not contain a cartridge, but the hammer was in the cocked position. He removed the cartridge case from the right barrel, later handing it to Detective Sergeant Lewis. As this was going on PC Sampson could see Mabel Attrill walking about in the back yard.

He then went back into the scullery and examined the body. He noticed that the clothing was not in any way disarranged. He found a hole through the lower left edge of the waistcoat. About six inches from the centre of the back there was a corresponding hole through the waist of the trousers and the shirt and vest. The areas around the holes were soaked in blood, and there was also a pool of blood on the rug on which the body was lying.

PC Sampson noticed a floorcloth in the scullery. There were footmarks on the floor, but he could see no signs of scratching or any evidence of a struggle having taken place. The other two rugs in the scullery were as normal and not rucked in any way.

PC Sampson spoke for the first time to Mabel about 20 minutes after his arrival. She was sitting on a sofa in the kitchen, looking very composed and not showing any sign of having been in a struggle. Mabel said to him: 'He threatened me by pointing the gun at me; I struggled with him and got it away. Somehow it went off, I did it in self-defence. I did not mean to kill him'.

PC Sampson then advised Mabel not to say any more about it, and arranged for Frank's body to be taken upstairs into a bedroom.

CHAPTER THREE

THE INVESTIGATION BEGINS

⌒

Having been called by the police, Dr Harold Frederic Bassano, who lived at Grove House, Alpine Road, Ventnor, arrived at East Appleford at ten o'clock and examined the body of Frank Cave in a bedroom of the farmhouse. He found a gunshot wound in the left loin, behind and exactly over the left kidney and below the level of the twelfth rib. It was egg shaped, with the apex upward, measuring some three inches in length and just over two in breadth. The wound appeared to be pointing upwards towards the chest, as if the shot had entered in an upward direction. The kidney was plainly visible inside the wound. Dr Bassano formed the opinion that the muzzle of the gun must have been at least six feet away from the deceased when it was discharged.

Around a quarter to eleven, Acting Detective Inspector Francis Rugman, stationed at Ventnor, arrived at the farm. He went upstairs and looked at the body, finding a wound in the back. He also looked at Mr Cave's clothing and found holes through various items.

He then examined the rest of the house. In particular he studied the rug in the scullery bearing what appeared to be bloodstains and the twelve-bore shotgun in the porch near the back door.

Around 1.30 that afternoon, Detective Sergeant Wallace Lewis arrived from Police Headquarters in Newport to see the body. He took various photographs in and around the house. It was now apparent to the officers that they were investigating a crime scene.

About three o'clock in the afternoon, Detective Inspector Rugman asked Mabel to sit in the kitchen, as he wanted to ask her some questions. Mabel was then cautioned, and DI Rugman said to her: 'I have seen the dead body of Frank Cave, who died of a gunshot wound received in the house. Can you give me any information as to how Mr Cave met his death?'

Mabel replied: 'The two children were in bed. We were just quarrelling. He got the gun out and loaded it and threatened me. I struggled to get it away from him. It went off and I don't know who is to blame.'

Detective Inspector Rugman then said to Mabel 'I have seen a double-barrelled shotgun standing in the scullery porch, can you tell me who put it there?' She replied, 'I must have put it outside. I took it away from him in the struggle and put it in the porch'.

DI Rugman again cautioned her and said that he was arresting her for the murder of Frank Cave. Mabel was then taken to Ventnor Police Station and charged 'that on the 20th October 1940, she did in the parish of Godshill in the Isle of Wight and County of Southampton murder Frank Cave, contrary to the Offences Against the Persons Act 1861, Sections 1–3'. In response Mabel said, 'I do not wish to say anything'.

The next day Dr Bassano examined Mabel at Ventnor Police Station. She had complained of stiffness on the right side of her neck and said that it hurt her to turn her head to the left. On examination of her neck the doctor could find no trace of any bruise or other injury. He found a trivial bruise at the outer edge of the left upper eyelid, while exactly underneath this bruise on the eyeball, just in the superficial tissues, was a small haemorrhage. He also found a very slight abrasion on the outer edge of the right eyelid, but this was so small as to be of no importance.

CHAPTER FOUR

POST MORTEM AND INQUEST

❧

Two days after the shooting, on Tuesday 22nd October, Dr Bassano assisted Sir Bernard Spilsbury in carrying out a post mortem examination on Frank Cave at Ventnor Mortuary.

The examination was in expert hands. Sir Bernard Spilsbury was Britain's leading forensic pathologist during much of the first half of the 20th century, acquiring a reputation especially by the press as 'the most brilliant scientific detective of all time'. He achieved a great deal in the advancement of forensic medicine, especially the use of this science in criminal trials.

Born in 1877, he read Natural Science at Magdalen College Oxford and then went on to St Mary's Hospital, London, in 1899. It may have been the gift of a microscope from his father that prompted him to switch from general practice to pathology, but it certainly changed his life and those of many others. Within a few years he became the chief pathologist at St Mary's and in 1908 he married Margaret Edith Horton. However it was the case of Dr Crippen in 1910 that elevated Spilsbury to celebrity status.

In 1907 Dr Hawley Harvey Crippen arrived in London from his home in Michigan, USA, together with his wife, a not very successful music hall singer, who was using the stage name Belle Elmore. Early in 1910, Belle disappeared. When anyone enquired about her, Crippen informed them that she had return to the States. However concern heightened when Ethel Le Neve, Crippen's former typist and now mistress, was seen wearing some of Belle's jewellery.

Soon rumours of Belle's disappearance reached the ears of the police and an investigation was launched. Upon searching Crippen's house, they found portions of a body buried in the basement. Meanwhile Crippen and Ethel Le Neve, who was disguised as a boy, had boarded the *SS Montrose*, sailing out of Antwerp headed for Quebec, Canada. The captain of the vessel, whose suspicions had been aroused by the couple, had used the newly invented telegraph to notify the authorities. At the end of July the couple were arrested and brought back to England, the first time the new wireless system had been used in connection with an arrest. This caused considerable press coverage and public interest.

Subsequently, at the Old Bailey, Crippen and Le Neve were tried separately for murder. Spilsbury's evidence especially concerned a small portion of human skin from the stomach, which according to him indicated an appendix scar; Belle Elmore had had an appendix operation. This was enough for the jury, and Crippen was hanged at Pentonville Prison in November of that year. Ethel Le Neve was acquitted.

The Crippen case established Spilsbury as the number one police pathologist in England. After the trial, he was appointed honorary pathologist to the Home Office. His fame continued and he was involved with numerous highly publicised murder trials in England and Wales, including the Brides in the Bath case and the Brighton Trunk Murders.

In 1920, while continuing his work for the Home Office, he was appointed lecturer on Morbid Anatomy and Histology at St. Bartholomew's Hospital.

Spilsbury became a kind of superhero, someone who could solve murders through pure science. He became a household name, with charisma to match. Over six feet tall and good-looking, he dressed immaculately and was rarely seen without a top hat and tails and sporting a buttonhole. In 1923 he was honoured with a knighthood.

Latterly, Sir Bernard was instrumental in the establishment of the first Police Scientific Department at Hendon and the setting up of Home Office Laboratories in other parts of the country, together with leading the General Medical Council and universities in an expansion of the teaching of forensic medicine.

Sir Bernard lived at 31 Marlborough Hill, London NW8, with his wife Edith and their children from 1912 until the Blitz in the autumn of 1940, just before the trial of Mabel Attrill.

★ ★ ★ ★ ★

At an Occasional Court held at Ventnor on Monday 21st October, before A J Sharpe Esq, Mabel was charged 'that she did feloniously kill and slay Frank Cave by shooting him in the back with a shotgun at about 7.30 am on Sunday 20th October 1940'.

Detective Inspector Rugman said that he had visited East Appleford Farm the previous day and seen the body of Frank

Cave, who had died from a gunshot wound. As a result of his enquiries he had arrested the prisoner and taken her to Ventnor Police Station, where she was cautioned and charged. In reply she had said, 'I do not wish to say anything'. The Inspector asked for her remand in custody to Holloway Prison until the 2nd November, and said that she would apply for legal aid. The application was granted.

The following Thursday, an inquest into the death of Frank Cave was conducted by Mr F A Joyce, Deputy Coroner, at the Upper Ventnor Methodist School. The Coroner sat with a jury, of whom Mr F G Webb was the foreman. Superintendent Morrison and Acting Inspector Rugman represented the Police, with Mr G S Green appearing for Frank Cave's widow Beatrice.

Supt. Morrison suggested to the Coroner that only evidence as to identification and the cause of death should be taken, as a suspect had been arrested and charged with murder.

Beatrice Cave stated that she lived with her married daughter, Doris Whittington, at No 4 East Appleford Cottages, just across the road from the farmhouse. She had been married to Frank Cave for over forty years, and had lived with him until six years ago. She added that Frank was 61 years old.

Doris Whittington stated that she was the daughter of Frank Cave. She said that on the Sunday morning she had heard a tap on the door and was told that her father had been shot. She then went into his house and found him lying full length on the floor with both arms by his side. She had put her arm under his head, when he had taken his last breath and died.

Dr Arthur Stratton said that he had been called around 7.45 am on Sunday and arrived at the farmhouse at 8.12. He had examined Mr Cave and found him to be dead. He did not know whether he had been moved, but found him lying on his back in the scullery with his feet towards the sink and his head towards the inner door. He saw a wound in the left loin, which appeared to have been caused by a shotgun.

Dr Harold Bassano said that on Tuesday he had assisted Sir Bernard Spilsbury at the post mortem examination. He had previously seen the body of Frank Cave at the farmhouse. The cause of death was the discharge from a sporting gun, the actual cause of death being shock and haemorrhage. The shot had penetrated the loin exactly over the left kidney. He had no hesitation in saying that the cause of death was as he had stated, and that the deceased must have lived at least five minutes after the shot was fired. He also found one or two slight bruises, one on the left side of the nose, the other on the leg, but these had nothing to do with his death and could have been caused by the deceased falling.

Mr Joyce, the Deputy Coroner, said that as someone had been arrested and charged with murder he could not admit any questions apart from those relating to the cause of death. He added that he was satisfied that this had been clearly established by the evidence of Dr Bassano. Speaking to the jury, he enquired whether he should discharge them or adjourn the inquiry. In reply the solicitor, Mr Green, said that if he discharged the jury he would have the option of calling them again. The Coroner replied that it might not be convenient to some of them.

The foreman of the jury rose to his feet and stated that they were all Ventnor men and were not likely to leave the Island.

The Coroner then replied that he could not see how they could render any further useful service. He continued by saying that the next course would be an appearance before a criminal court and that he was relying on the fact that there must be a committal. The cause of death in his opinion had been proved, and accordingly there would not be a verdict.

The inquiry was adjourned and the jury were discharged. The foreman, Mr Webb, handed the jurors' fees to Beatrice, but she said she would rather they were given to the Police Fund.

The next day Frank was buried at Carisbrooke Cemetery, following a service at St John's Church, Newport, where the vicar, The Rev W H Mackinnon, officiated. The family mourners included Frank's three sons, Charles, Frederick and Teddy, all in Army uniform; his daughter Doris; his sister Rose and her husband; and his two brothers Edward and William with their respective wives. Among those also attending included representatives from Newport Conservative Club and from the auctioneers at Newport cattle market.

On Saturday 2nd November at the Isle of Wight County Petty Sessions, sitting at the Guildhall, Newport, before Alderman A Andrews, an application was made by Superintendent Morrison that Mabel Attrill, charged with the murder of Frank Cave, should be remanded until November 12th. Superintendent Morrison said that it was hoped the Director of Public Prosecutions would be able to proceed when the prisoner appeared before the County Magistrates at Ryde on that date. The application was granted.

CHAPTER FIVE

COMMITTED FOR TRIAL

∽

On Tuesday 12th November 1940 at The Isle of Wight County Bench sitting in Ryde, Mabel Attrill appeared on remand charged with the murder of her employer Frank Cave. She was neatly dressed in a black hat and grey coat and pleaded not guilty to the charge. A Mr H Palmer legally represented Mabel.

The chairman of the magistrates was Sir Godfrey Baring, sitting with a full complement of eight other magistrates, comprising four former senior army officers and four local businessmen. Maybe at the time the constitution of the bench, being solely male, was not unusual for the trial of a young woman.

Sir Godfrey Baring had a distinguished record of public service on the Island. He was born in 1871 and in 1911 he had been created 1st Baronet Baring of Nubia House, Cowes. As a Liberal, Sir Godfrey stood for Parliament in 1906, his victory ending a line of 25 Conservative MPs on the Island. He remained MP for the Isle of Wight until 1910, when he became MP for Barnstaple in Devon, holding the seat until 1918. He had been Chairman of Isle of Wight County Council since 1898.

Opening the case for the Director of Public Prosecutions, Mr J F Claxton said the facts of the case were straightforward.

He went on to outline how Herbert Smith had heard a gunshot around 7.30 on the morning of Sunday 20th October, while milking the cows. He had found a double-barrelled shotgun standing on its butt in the porch and seen the accused standing near the door. Mr Claxton then went on to explain how Doris Whittington had been awoken by a tap on her door and on opening it she saw the accused, who had simply said 'Come quick, the old man is shot'. He described how Doris had run across the road and found her father lying on his back in the scullery, and said that when she had asked the accused how it happened, she had replied: 'We were struggling and the gun went off; it was either him or me. He loaded the gun and meant it for me. He took a few steps after he was shot and got to the sink'.

Mr Claxton then said to the court: 'You will see that at the first opportunity the accused said there was a struggle, but Mrs Whittington will tell you that when she saw Miss Attrill she was perfectly composed, that her hair was in no way disarranged and her clothes showed no signs of a struggle'. Mr Claxton then went on to say that the scullery, which she had entered almost immediately after the incident, was in no way untidy, and there would be police evidence that they could find nothing to show that there had been a struggle.

Mr Claxton continued by saying that the accused had a small smear of blood on her thumb, and had stated 'it was all over a quarrel through that party coming rabbiting'. That party, said Mr Claxton, referred to a Mrs Evans. The accused had been living in the same house as Frank Cave, as his housekeeper, while his wife, from whom he was separated, was living in another house. Although it was not for the prosecution to prove a motive, the Bench might think that the possible motive was jealousy, for there could be little doubt that the accused was jealous of Mrs Evans coming rabbiting.

Kenneth Edward Souter, architect and surveyor, of 11 Lind Street, Ryde, produced a plan he had made at a request of the police of the house at East Appleford Farm.

In giving evidence Detective Sergeant Lewis produced a number of photographs he had taken, having the untouched negatives in his possession. From these negatives he had prepared photographic enlargements, and he produced a book of exhibits. They included a picture of the gun standing in the porch, the bloodstained mat in the scullery and a box of cartridges standing in the bottom left corner of a glass cupboard. In addition he showed a photograph of a police officer, namely PC Sampson, lying as near as possible in the position in which the dead man was found.

DS Lewis said that he had measured the size of the scullery and found it to be just over 12 feet by 11 feet. He had examined the scullery but could find no evidence that would support the suggestion that there had been a struggle.

Doris Whittington next gave evidence as to how she had seen her father lying on the scullery floor in a pool of blood. Having telephoned the doctor and the police, she had noticed the accused, who was walking about doing her household duties. She was not crying and her clothes and hair were not disarranged. Later in the morning, around 11 o'clock, she recalled seeing Mrs Evans in her car outside the farm, but did not speak to her.

Dr James Davidson, Director of the Metropolitan Police

Laboratory at Hendon, informed the Court that on the 28th October he had received various items of evidence from the Isle of Wight Police in relation to the death of Frank Cave, including clothing, a double-barrelled twelve-bore shotgun and a box of cartridges. He had examined the deceased's clothing and found that the waistcoat showed a gunshot hole about one and a half inches by one and three quarters in size which interrupted the lower margin at the back and was three and half inches from the middle seam. The margins were irregular and one or two small pellet holes could be seen near the margin. There was no evidence of burning of the cloth or unburnt powder, and bloodstaining was present.

Dr Davidson continued his evidence in relation to the dead man's trousers, shirt and vest, where a gunshot hole was found, with considerable bloodstaining, but again there was no evidence of burning of the cloth or of unburnt powder.

He went on to tell the court that he had carried out tests on the shotgun and the box of cartridges taken from the farm. He fired them from successive distances from one foot up to seven feet into pieces of calico-covered card supported in a frame. The results of the experiment showed that firing of the right-hand barrel at a distance of six feet produced an effect similar to that found on the clothing. In addition he tested the spread of the shot and the presence or absence of burning or of unburnt powder. Dr Davidson concluded that the shotgun in this case was fired at the deceased man from a distance of about six feet. He then explained that he had tested the pull of the triggers of the gun, both of which he found to be heavier than normal, the pull on the right trigger being just under eight pounds and that of the left to be six and a half pounds. The weight of the gun was seven and a quarter pounds. He stated that the normal pull should be slightly less than half the weight of the gun.

On cross-examination by Mr Palmer, Dr Davidson explained that he had fired at right angles into the calico and directly opposite. He did not fire more than one cartridge at any given distance, as he did not think it desirable to do so as the results were conclusive. The cartridges had the appearance to him of being new, but he did not examine them to see if they were all of the same age.

The next person to be called to the witness stand was 41-year-old Mrs Evans. She gave her full name to be Ellen Lilian May Evans, living at Standen Heath, Staplers, just north east of Newport. She said she was a married woman whose husband was serving in the armed forces, and she was currently employed as a land girl. She continued to say that she had known Frank Cave since just before Christmas 1939, and had been in the habit of rabbiting with ferrets with her stepbrother Albert Pike and that sometimes Frank Cave's son Charles would come with them. They always went to East Appleford and would start off from the farm.

She said that sometimes Frank would accompany them, but she had never seen him with a gun and did not know he had one. Mrs Evans went on to say that she had left off rabbiting about the beginning of April, and did not continue to go to the farm after rabbiting had finished, when she had started her job as a land girl. She said that except for the sport of rabbiting and going to the farm she did not really know the deceased, and that he never used to come and visit her.

On the 13th October Mrs Evans had gone down to Frank Cave's farm to look at a German bomber that had been brought down. There she had seen Frank with two other men, and had arranged at that meeting to go rabbiting on the following Sunday. On that Sunday, the 20th October, she went by car accompanied by her stepbrother, stopping outside the farm. There she spoke to Mrs Beatrice Cave, who told her what had happened. Mrs Evans concluded her evidence by saying that she had not known the accused until she had started to go out to the farm, and she knew her as well as she knew Mr Frank Cave.

Mr Claxton, for the DPP, said that he was not going to call Sir Bernard Spilsbury, who had made the post mortem, but would submit a statutory declaration of his evidence and call him at a later date.

Mr Palmer informed the Bench that Miss Attrill would reserve her defence.

After an all-day hearing the Bench retired. On their return they committed Mabel Attrill for trial at Winchester Assizes, upon which Mr Palmer applied, under the Poor Prisoners Defence Regulations, for a defence certificate and for two counsels to be briefed. Both applications were granted. Mabel was remanded and returned to Holloway Prison.

CHAPTER SIX

A VITAL PRECEDENT

The building where Mabel Attrill was to be tried had a long and colourful history, dating back more than 700 years. Building on Winchester Castle's Great Hall began in 1222 and was completed some thirteen years later. It became the setting for many councils and parliaments, and was the place where travelling justices would try cases from the Hampshire area.

Over the centuries the Great Hall had seen numerous famous trials, especially that in 1603 of Sir Walter Raleigh – the charge against him of high treason was heard at Winchester because of the plague in London.

In 1647, while Charles I was imprisoned in Carisbrooke Castle, Captain John Burleigh was tried on a charge of attempting to raise forces and rescue him. He pleaded not guilty, but was convicted and sentenced to be hanged, drawn and quartered.

Numerous high-profile cases occurred some forty years later during the reign of the Catholic James II, when a rebellion led by the illegitimate son of Charles II, the Duke of Monmouth, was ended at the battle of Sedgemoor. What followed in the Great Hall and other major towns in the South

26

East Appleford Farm

William and Edward Cave

East Appleford Cottages

Sir Bernard Spilsbury

Sir Godfrey Baring

Shot gun standing in the porch

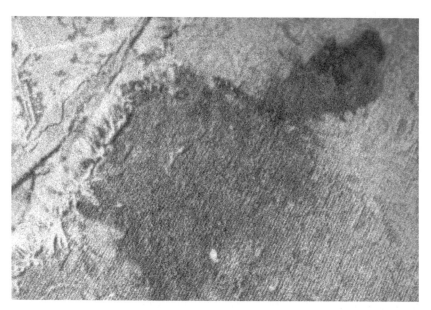

Bloodstained mat in scullery

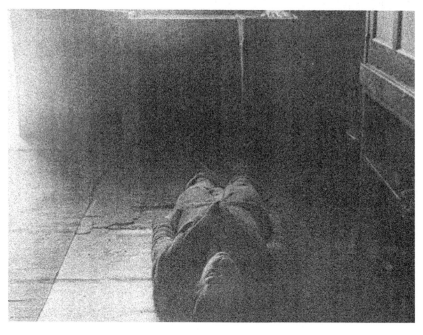

PC Sampson laying in position in which Frank Cave was found.

J D Casswell

Daily Express

TODAY'S WEATHER : SHOWERS.   RADIO PROGRAMMES : PAGE 17.

NO. 10,889   SATURDAY, APRIL 6, 1935   ONE PENNY

LAW GIVES A MAN BACK HIS LI[FE]

Peers Quash Death Sentence—For First Time In Histor[y]

"I'm happy to be free again."   "Now for a biscuit and cup of tea."

"It's great to light a pipe again."   "I knew that justice would prevail."

Exclusive "Daily Express" camera studies of Reginald Woolmington after his release

"But—I shall miss my w[ife]"

Secrets Of The Mind

LOOK out on Monday for the "Daily Express" Literacy Course No. 2.

The first course, recently completed, was enormously popular.

The second is more advanced. You will learn how your Mind develops; how good and bad habits are formed; secrets of judgment and will-power.

Begin the course on Monday.

MR. EDEN RETURNS

LORDS SAVE A LABOURER

A Warder Shook His Hand—Then He Asked For His Pipe

FOR THE FIRST TIME IN HISTORY A MAN WHO HAD BEEN CONDEMNED TO DIE WAS SET FREE YESTERDAY BY A DECISION OF THE HOUSE OF LORDS.

Reginald Woolmington, a twenty-one-year-old Somerset farm labourer, had been accused of the murder by shooting of his girl-wife...

WINIFRED BARNES IS DEAD

£13,000,000 BETS IN FIVE DAYS

BOOKMAKERS have made up their accounts for the first five days of the racing season at Lincoln and Liverpool. These show that at least £13,000,000 has been spent in betting

GERMAN WO[MEN]

M.P.s DEMAND A[CTION]

PUBLIC uneasiness has been increased by the revelation that Dr. Doris Fabian at Great Ormond-street, W.C., was engaged in active anti-Nazi propaganda in England from the first in 1933.

It was definitely established yesterday that since that time both had been intriguing here against the Nazi Government. Both had taken an active part in exposing the activities of Nazi agents in London.

LATE

U.S. PU[BLIC]

TA[...]

Reginald Woolmington

Dorothy O'Grady

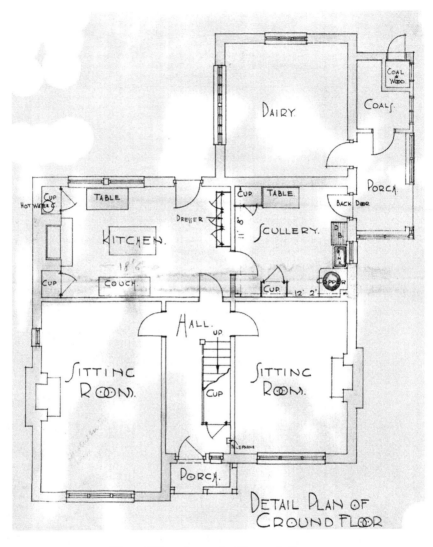

Plan of Farmhouse by Kenneth Souter

was known as the Bloody Assizes, thanks to the hundreds of death sentences handed down by Judge Jeffreys.

Over the next couple of centuries the Great Hall continued to be one of the major courthouses in the South of England. In 1830 there was considerable civil unrest and rioting because of shortages of food and a lack of jobs. As a result 245 persons were tried at a Special Assizes in the Great Hall, and 95 of them were sentenced to death. Eventually only two were hanged, the remainder being transported to Australia.

In 1874 new law courts were built and the Great Hall ceased to be used for trials. However the new building had been built over a ditch that had surrounded the castle and it began to subside, to be finally demolished in 1937. The Great Hall was reinstated as a seat of justice, and once again it became the setting for the Assizes. It was here that Mabel found herself in the December of 1940.

The Hampshire Autumn Assizes opened in Winchester on the 6th December 1940 before the Hon. Sir Malcolm Martin Macnaughton KBE.

Sir Malcolm, born 1869, was the fourth son of Baron Edward Macnaughton, who had been a barrister and Conservative Member of Parliament for Antrim. Until his death in 1913 he had been a Law Lord in the Court of Appeal. Sir Malcolm had followed in his father's footsteps, being called to the Bar at Lincoln's Inn in 1894, serving as Member of Parliament for Londonderry from 1922 until 1928, and then being appointed Judge of the King's Bench Division of the High Court.

Because of the volume of court work, Mabel Attrill's case

did not begin until the 16th of December. In the meantime, thanks to the closely-adjoining cells, news spread quickly among the remand prisoners. It was not long before Mabel discovered that another Isle of Wight woman was also awaiting trial for her life – in her case, for spying.

The case which preceded hers that day must have filled Mabel with a sense of impending doom. Dorothy Pamela O'Grady aged 42, married and living in Sandown, had pleaded not guilty to nine counts under the Treachery Act 1940, the Official Secrets Act 1911 and the Defence Regulations 1939, for offences allegedly committed between August and September 1940 on the Island. The trial took place in camera, as Dorothy was being tried as a spy.

The jury were absent for an hour and on their return found her not guilty of the first count of conspiracy with a person or persons unknown to impede the operations of HM Forces or to assist the enemy, but guilty of counts charging her with making sketch maps and doing acts to assist the enemy.

As the penalty imposed by the Treachery Act, under which she had been found guilty, was the death penalty, Sir Malcolm donned the black cap and pronounced a sentence of death by hanging. All in the court stood. Later Dorothy O'Grady's sentence would be commuted to a prison term, but neither Mabel Attrill nor anyone else knew that at the time.

* * * * *

At the opening of Mabel's trial, she pleaded not guilty to the charge of murdering Frank Cave. Joshua Casswell KC and Mr

Munro Kerr represented her. For the prosecution on behalf of The Director of Public Prosecutions were Mr J G Trapnell KC and Mr J Scott Henderson. The jury consisted of ten men and two women.

Mabel Attrill's defence was in good hands with Joshua Casswell. He was born in the family home near Wimbledon Common in 1886, and continued to live there for much of his life. As a schoolboy he attended nearby King's College School and in 1905 he was awarded an open scholarship to Pembroke College, Oxford. His family had no legal connections, but the young Casswell thought a qualification as a barrister-at-law would stand him in good stead in obtaining an appointment in Government Service, especially in the Foreign Office.

In 1909 he came down from Oxford and spent six months in a solicitor's office in London before returning to Oxford to sit his Bar Final exams. In November 1910 he was called to the Bar in Middle Temple Hall. He then spent the next year in chambers as a 'pupil' before becoming a fully qualified barrister, and in February 1912 moved into chambers on the top floor of No 3 North, King's Bench Walk.

In August 1914 Great Britain and Germany were at war, and soon Casswell was invited to undertake the organisation of V Division of the Metropolitan Special Constabulary and bid farewell to his barrister's practice. A few months later he obtained a commission in the Horse Transport of the Army Service Corps. He saw active service in France, where in 1916 he was mentioned in despatches, and eventually was promoted to the rank of Major.

He was demobilized in March 1919 and returned to his

legal practice. In the April he married Irene Fitzroy and over the next ten years they had four children, a girl and three boys.

During the 1920s he undertook a variety of court work from his increasingly successful practice, and in 1928 he appeared for the Director of Public Prosecutions in a murder trial. The following year he conducted his first of many as counsel for the defence in a murder case.

In 1938 Casswell became a KC – King's Counsel – or 'took silk' as it is known, from the material of which the KC (now QC, Queen's Council) gown is made. By the time he retired in 1951, he had defended nearly 40 people charged with murder, only five of them being hanged. Many of these defendants were being represented under the Poor Prisoners' Defence Regulations, which meant that his fee, at the time of Mabel Attrill's case, amounted to only £3 5s. 6d. (£3.27p) for the first day, and £2 4s. 6d. (£2.22) for each subsequent day, together with a daily travelling allowance of £1 1s. 6d. (£1.7p), provided he lived more than twenty miles from the court. The work he undertook was obviously not for financial reward.

This was not the first time Joshua Casswell and John Trapnell had locked horns in the courtroom; most notably they had clashed five years earlier, in a House of Lords appeal case which had become arguably the most important case on evidence in English criminal law, namely *Woolmington v Director of Public Prosecutions 1935*. Joshua Casswell was acting on behalf of Reginald Woolmington and John Trapnell for the DPP. The facts of this case bore a resemblance to what happened at East Appleford nearly six years later, but the consequences for English law were irrevocable.

In January 1935 at the Somerset Winter Assizes, situated in Taunton, Reginald Woolmington was charged with murdering his wife Violet Kathleen Woolmington. The couple had married in August 1934. He was a 21-year-old farm labourer and Violet was 17. They lived at Castleton, near Sherborne in Dorset, on the farm of Reginald's employer, a Mr Cheeseman. On the 14th October Violet gave birth to a child. But in November, less than three months into matrimony, she left Reginald and went to live with her mother in Milborne Port. He wanted her to go back to him and made efforts to induce her to do so, but she would not.

Before the marriage Violet had worked in the family home in Milborne Port with her widowed mother, Mrs Lilian Smith, in the local industry of home glove making. The glove factories contracted out their work to women living in the surrounding area, who made up the gloves in their own homes on a piece-rate basis, earning themselves a good and regular income.

Mrs Smith felt the loss of Violet's contribution to the family income, and made her feelings known. Shortly after the birth of the Woolmingtons' baby son she started visiting her daughter, taking with her bundles of unmade-up gloves, which they both worked on. Reginald felt that his mother-in-law had intentionally attempted to induce Violet to leave him and return to live with her, a fact that Lilian Smith emphatically denied during cross-examination by Casswell.

Reginald Woolmington thought that he might frighten his wife into obedience by threatening to shoot himself. So on the morning of the 10th December he took a shotgun belonging to Mr Cheeseman and two cartridges from a box nearby. With a fretsaw, he then sawed off part of the barrels and loaded the gun with the two cartridges. He attached some electrical flex to the gun, and with this he suspended the gun from his shoulder under his overcoat. He then cycled to the home of his mother-in-law, where he confronted Violet.

She said that she would not go back to him, and was intending to go into domestic service. Woolmington said that if she would not come back to him he would shoot himself. To explain how he meant to do it, he unbuttoned his overcoat and brought the gun across his waist. The gun went off; according to Woolmington, he did not know it was pointing at his wife. Violet was shot through the heart and killed. When the police arrived he was taken to the police station, where he was charged. Reginald's only reply was 'I want to say nothing, except that I did it, and they can do what they like. It was jealousy I suppose. Her mother enticed her away from me. I done all I could to get her back, that's all'.

Casswell had obtained evidence from an expert gunsmith that the shotgun's trigger pull was exceptionally light and therefore more likely to have been fired by mischance.

On questioning Woolmington in the witness box, Casswell asked what had happened that morning. He replied 'I had no intention of killing Violet when I went to Milborne Port'. His sole objective was to frighten her into coming back by threatening to kill himself. 'When she wouldn't come with me I brought the gun up across my waist from under my overcoat to show her that I was serious about taking my own life. As I pulled the gun round it went off, and Violet fell. I swear my finger never touched the trigger'.

Casswell felt that Woolmington's account of the events had an effect upon some of the jurors, and although there was a rigorous cross-examination by John Trapnell for the prosecution, a different atmosphere pervaded the court.

As Casswell was to report later, only two people had been present in the kitchen on the morning of the 10th December. One of them was now dead, and the other was standing in the court, composed and calm in the witness box, saying that her death was an accident. Who was to deny the truth of his claim?

Mr Justice Finlay summed up the facts of the case and the jury went out to consider their verdict. One hour, twenty-five minutes later they returned, unable to agree. The foreman of the jury told the judge 'we have been through it thoroughly... we could not agree if we sat until tomorrow morning'. Casswell was convinced that should they have convicted, an appeal would have been fruitless, as he could see no fault in the judge's summing up.

Mr Justice Finlay ordered a new trial to take place the following month at Bristol Assizes. The presiding judge would be Mr Justice Rigby Swift.

On the 14th February 1935 at Bristol Assize Court, Reginald Woolmington returned to the dock and the retrial commenced. The evidence followed the same pattern as the first trial, but the difference lay in the summing-up by the judge Mr Justice Swift.

The judge proceeded to outline the facts of the case, and then produced a copy of *Archbold's Criminal Pleadings*, the bible for all criminal lawyers. He then read a passage from the book:

'All homicide is presumed to be malicious, and murder, unless the

contrary appears from circumstances of alleviation, excuse or justification. In every charge of murder, the fact of the killing being first proved, all the circumstances of accident, necessity, or infirmity, are to be satisfactorily proved by the prisoner, unless they arise out of the evidence produced against him, for the law presumeth the fact to have been founded in malice until the contrary appeareth.'

The Judge then went on to explain to the jury what this meant in ordinary terms. He said: 'If once you find that a person has been guilty of killing another, it is for the person who has been guilty to satisfy you that the crime is something less than the murder with which he has been charged'.

The Judge was informing the jury that in effect it was for Woolmington to prove that Violet's death was accidental and not the prosecution's duty to prove it was not.

The jury took only an hour and nine minutes to return a verdict of guilty, and Woolmington was sentenced to death.

Casswell had long thought that the passage from *Archbold*, based on previous legal authority found in *Foster's Crown Law* dating back to 1762, was incorrect, as it seemed to go against the whole foundation of English criminal law, that a man is presumed innocent until he is proved guilty and that it is the duty of the prosecution to prove that guilt. Accordingly Casswell advised Woolmington to appeal, although he realised that the fundamentally conservative establishment would be loath to admit that a statement of law that had stood for nearly two hundred years was incorrect. But Casswell was convinced he was right.

Woolmington applied for leave to appeal against his conviction, and on the 18th March 1935 the case was heard at the Court of Criminal Appeal in the Strand, before Mr Justice Avory, Mr Justice Lawrence and Mr Justice Greaves-Lord. Casswell relied upon the argument that the trial judge, Mr Justice Swift, had misdirected the jury by telling them that in the circumstances of the case he was presumed in law to be guilty of the murder unless he could satisfy the jury that his wife's death was due to an accident. Having been unable to prove his innocence, Woolmington had been convicted.

However the Court of Criminal Appeal refused the application, Mr Justice Avory saying 'There could be no question that the judge properly laid down the law applicable to this case'. Casswell argued that Swift should have told the jury that if they entertained reasonable doubt as to whether they should accept Woolmington's explanation of his wife's death, it was their duty to acquit, or at least convict of manslaughter only. To this Mr Justice Avory replied that even if such direction were given, the jury would still inevitably have convicted the prisoner.

To Casswell this seemed blatantly unjust. At the first trial Mr Justice Findlay had directed the jury in exactly the same terms as he had suggested Mr Justice Swift should have done at the second trial. The jury had not 'inevitably' convicted him then; in fact they had failed to agree. Casswell felt so strongly about the case that although his instructions had finished, he applied to the Attorney General to allow the case to be taken to the House of Lords, as he thought it was his duty to submit that the point of law involved was so important as to justify this.

The Attorney General certified that the decision of the Court of Criminal Appeal involved a point of law of exceptional public importance and that, in his opinion, it was desirable in the public interest that a further appeal should be brought, and the appeal was allowed to be brought before the House of Lords. This was the first time an Attorney General's fiat had been granted to a defendant in a murder case since the Court of Criminal Appeal was set up in 1907.

Several days before the hearing started in the House of Lords, Lord Sankey, Lord Chancellor, decided that a King's Counsel should be briefed to lead the defence, and Terence O'Connor KC was appointed, with Joshua Casswell as his junior.

On the 4th April proceedings commenced, Terence O'Connor KC and Joshua Casswell presenting their legal arguments for the defence before five Law Lords. The following day John Trapnell KC and Reginald Knight presented their arguments for the prosecution. At the end of that day the hearing eventually finished when the Lord Chancellor, Viscount Lord Sankey, announced the decision on the presumption of innocence, which reversed the then legal wisdom stretching back some 175 years: *'Throughout the web of the English Criminal Law one golden thread is always to be seen, that it is the duty of the prosecution to prove the prisoner's guilt.'*

Thus if, as Reginald Woolmington had claimed, the death of his wife at his hands when the shotgun went off was an accident, it was for the prosecution to disprove this theory beyond reasonable doubt, not for the prisoner to persuade the jury on the balance of probabilities to accept the truth of his explanation.

The conviction was quashed, Woolmington was acquitted, and the law was rewritten.

CHAPTER SEVEN

TRIAL AND VERDICT

❧

And so on the 16th December 1940 at Winchester Assizes, John Trapnell opened the case for the prosecution by informing the Court that the accused had for about five years been living at East Appleford Farm, as a housekeeper of the deceased, a farmer. His wife had left him before the accused went to work at the farm and latterly had been living with one of her daughters quite close to the farm. About 7.40 on the morning of Sunday 20th October, the accused had appeared at the daughter's cottage and in an agitated voice had said 'Come quick, the old man has been shot!' or words to that effect.

The daughter had followed the accused over to the farm and there found the deceased lying on his back in the scullery, and as she lifted his head he had breathed his last. The police and doctor were summoned by telephone and it was found that the deceased had a large wound in his back, obviously a gunshot wound, while an old pattern double-barrelled shotgun containing one spent cartridge was standing in a corner of the porch a few feet from the body. Sir Bernard Spilsbury, assisted by Dr Bassano, on behalf of The Director of Public Prosecutions, carried out a post mortem examination.

Sir Bernard gave his address as being 1 Verulam Buildings, Grays Inn, London WC1, and stated that he was a registered medical practitioner and honorary pathologist to the Home Office. On Tuesday 22nd October 1940, at the mortuary in Ventnor, he had conducted a post-mortem examination of the body of a man in the presence of Dr Bassano and police officers. He found that the body was that of a well-nourished man, five feet two inches in height. Rigor mortis and hypostatic staining were present. Decomposition was present around the wound in the back, with gas production beneath the skin.

He found a gunshot wound in the lower part of the back of the trunk on the left side. The wound was elliptical in shape, measuring three inches vertically by two and a quarter inches horizontally in its widest part. At its upper end the wound was slightly undercut. The edge of the wound was slightly crenated in places, and in its upper part on each side were several tiny separate wounds close to the main wound. The centre of the wound was three feet seven inches above ground when in a standing position. A mass of kidney projected through the wound. There was no blackening or other change in the skin round the wound.

Sir Bernard continued his evidence on the external appearance of the body by stating that there was a small abrasion with a bruise beneath it on the left side of the bridge of the nose, and a small bruise on the right shin.

Sir Bernard then went on with his evidence concerning the internal examination of the body by stating that he found the main direction of the shot that entered the body through the wound in the left back was directly forwards and upwards.

The mass of shot had produced a large ragged wound in the upper part of the left kidney, another near the upper end of the spleen and another in the lower part of the left lung. Several shot were found in the left portion of the pancreas. Three wads from the cartridge were in the wound, and the stomach wall had been pierced, five shot being found within the stomach and two in its wall. There were several shot holes in the lower surface of the left lobe of the liver and one in the left wall of the heart, with a number in the main artery, the aorta, in the lower part of the chest. Shot was also found free in the left pleural cavity and in the left chest wall, in the loose tissues around the injured aorta and kidney and in the bottom of the left lung.

As for the general condition of the deceased, Sir Bernard concluded that for his age he had been a healthy man, and there was no natural disease that caused or contributed to his death. The cause of death was shock and loss of blood due to a gunshot wound in the back.

The width of the wound of two and quarter inches indicated to Sir Bernard that the mass of shot had had room to spread out after leaving the muzzle of the weapon, and the tiny separate wounds were produced by isolated shot which had spread further. This indicated that the muzzle of the weapon could not have been close to the body at the time of discharge. In his opinion the shortest distance at which the weapon could have been discharged was five to six feet, and it might have been more.

From the structures that were penetrated it was clear that the shot had a fairly marked upward direction. If the deceased had been standing upright when he was shot, the wound being three feet seven inches from ground level, the weapon must have been pointed at an angle upwards. It was doubtful whether at a range of five to six feet the wound could have been inflicted as it was, even if the butt of the weapon was on the ground. In Sir Bernard's opinion the deceased must have been bending forward when the weapon was fired behind him. The distance from which the weapon must have been fired rendered it impossible for the wound to have been self-inflicted or to have occurred in the course of a struggle between two persons for possession of the weapon.

Sir Bernard concluded his evidence by stating that from the position of the deceased's body and the distribution of blood on the floor, it was his opinion that the deceased was bending over the sink in the scullery when he was shot from behind at a range of least five to six feet, and that he collapsed at once and fell on his back on the floor.

John Trapnell continued with the case for the prosecution, and called Frank's wife Beatrice to give evidence.

Beatrice said that she lived with her married daughter at the cottages opposite East Appleford Farm, and that Mabel Attrill had been living with her husband at the farmhouse since she had left him some six years before. She continued by saying that the previous May she had moved back into the matrimonial home for five or six weeks, on condition that Mabel Attrill went away to work. This Mabel did not do, and Beatrice, not being able to tolerate the situation, left her husband again. Beatrice had told Mabel to leave her husband, as women had always been his downfall, and that she had ten children, nine of whom were still living.

Beatrice was asked why she had left Frank originally. She replied that it had been because of his behaviour. He was especially quarrelsome when he had more drink than was good for him, usually after he had been to the cattle market in Newport.

She was then asked if he had ever hit her while they were living together. She replied that she had been hit on several occasions.

'Was it every week?'

'No, not every week, but a good many times.'

Doris Whittington, Frank's daughter, was then called to the stand. She told the court that on that Sunday morning she had been called by the accused and had found her father only just alive in the scullery of the farmhouse. She had seen a shotgun in the porch. She then telephoned the police.

Doris had noticed that Mabel seemed to be in a trance. She had asked her what had happened. In reply Mabel said: 'we were struggling and the gun went off; it was either him or me. Frank loaded the gun and meant it for me. We were quarrelling over a party coming rabbiting.'

On cross-examination, Casswell established from Doris that Frank Cave had previously threatened Mabel with the gun.

Dr Stratton then gave evidence describing the injuries he had found, and stated that Mabel Attrill had said to him: 'I struggled with him to get the gun away. Somehow it went off. I did it in self-defence; I did not mean to kill him'.

Acting Inspector Rugman was next to give his evidence, which was similar to the evidence given by Dr. Stratton, but he added that the accused had said 'I do not know who is to blame'.

The next to be called was Mrs Ellen Evans, who said she had been rabbiting at Frank Cave's farm, and on the 20th October she had gone there with her stepbrother at about 10.50 am. On cross-examination by Casswell, Mrs Evans denied that she had been out in a car with Frank Cave and that he had visited her at Arreton. She thought that Miss Attrill was Frank Cave's wife when she first went there.

Casswell asked Mrs Evans: 'Did you know that your association with Mr Cave was causing trouble between him and Miss Attrill?'

She replied that she did not, but she agreed that she had been in the farmhouse and had tea, and that sometimes Mr Cave would bring a cup of tea out in the middle of the day and take back the rabbits they had caught.

Dr Davidson from Hendon Metropolitan Police Laboratory and Dr Bassano then gave expert evidence, the latter expressing the opinion that the shot had been fired at a range of not less than six feet.

Joshua Casswell opened the case for the defence and contended that the tragedy was the result of an accident. The circumstances replicated the facts of *Woolmington v DPP (1935)*, and the House of Lords decision was abundantly clear, namely that the death of Frank Cave was at Mabel Attrill's hands when the shotgun went off as a result of an accident. It was for the prosecution to disprove this theory beyond reasonable doubt. This, Casswell maintained, had not been done. It was not for the defendant to convince the jury on the balance of probabilities to accept the truth of her explanation.

Mabel was called to the stand to give her evidence, saying

that she was 25 years of age and unmarried. Since 1935 she had been living at Appleford Farm with Mr Cave. She had first met him when he had an accident with his car, and after that went to work at his house on a daily basis, Mrs Cave having left by then. In March 1935 he took her out to a party and for the first time she had some intoxicating liquor. Then he had taken her back to the farmhouse instead of to her own home, but she could not remember much about it. Around 2.30 am he had taken her back to her home. She did not realise that he had been intimate with her, but the following December she had given birth to a baby girl. She had then gone to live with him at the farm. Before that he had paid her ten shillings a week, but afterwards he had reduced the payment to five shillings. In December 1936 she had a second baby girl, but this one died, in September 1937. There was a third baby, a boy, in March 1938, who was still alive. She said that Frank Cave was the father of the three children.

Mabel continued her evidence by saying that Frank Cave often had too much to drink and then became brutal towards her. He had more than once threatened her with a gun, and on one occasion she left him as a consequence. When he had returned from Newport Market she had said that she would leave him, and he replied that if she did he 'would do us all in'. She then went to her mother's house, but Frank would not let her take her son with her. She recollected that it was that particular day her mother had had to take the gun from him.

Casswell then asked Mabel about Mrs Evans. She replied that around Christmas last year Mrs Evans started coming to the farm ferreting almost every day, and sometimes Frank went with her. She did not approve of Mrs Evans, and told Frank so. She continued by saying that in early October of this year, Frank had successfully sold a good deal of stock at Newport Market. He seemed to be different, and she could not seem to please him. From the week beginning the 13th October she said Frank went out practically every evening, and it was evident when he came home that he had had a drink; he was not very kind to her.

On the afternoon of Sunday 13th October she had seen Mrs Evans at the farm in a car. The following Saturday, the 19th, when Frank returned home from the market, he was very quarrelsome. He said that he had met Mrs Evans in Newport and that she was coming out on Sunday rabbiting. Mabel said that she would speak to Mrs Evans as she did not approve, but according to Mabel, Frank replied that she would not have the chance. Later that evening he told her that he was going to ask Mrs Evans to come rabbiting all winter and give up her job. He said that he would not want dinner the next day, as he would be out all day. Mabel assumed that he would be going out with Mrs Evans.

Mabel continued her evidence by saying that she had got up around seven o'clock on the Sunday morning, Frank getting up a little later. She had cleaned the sitting-room grate and started work in the kitchen when a quarrel developed with Frank concerning Mrs Evans. When she had said that she would speak with 'that woman', Frank had become angry. Mabel alleged that Frank had struck her on the eye and grabbed her by the throat, the argument continuing for about ten minutes. Mabel then went from the kitchen back into the sitting room and continued to clean the grate.

She had then heard the glass door of the cabinet open, looked around and seen him with a gun pointing at her. Mabel said he did not say anything but he 'looked guilty' and she thought he meant to do her harm. She rushed towards him and he went into the scullery.

'I took the gun away from behind him, catching hold about the centre of it. I think I took it in my left hand. The gun came away quicker than I thought and I went backwards'.

Casswell asked Mabel: 'What was your idea in taking the gun away, why did you snatch the gun?'

'I took it from him to be on the safe side.'

'What is the next thing you knew?'

'I only know the gun went off.'

'Did you know the gun was loaded?'

'No, I did not.'

'Have you ever fired a gun?'

'I know nothing about guns.'

'What happened to Mr Cave when you took the gun away?'

'He went several steps forward.'

'What happened to the gun?'

'I fancy I dropped it, and I must have picked it up and put it in the corner as I went to fetch Mrs Doris Whittington.'

Mabel added that she had knelt down by him. When she saw his condition, she rushed out and went to Doris Whittington. Having given Doris the police station telephone number, Doris said that she could manage so long as she would keep the children quiet. She told Doris that during the quarrel Frank had her on the ground and was kneeling on her.

Casswell asked Mabel: 'Did you at any time mean the gun to go off?'

'No, definitely not.'

During cross examination by John Trapnell, Mabel said that as far as she knew the gun was not kept loaded, and that the trouble had really started because he had got up too early. She had the impression that Frank was 'carrying on' with Mrs Evans. It was his 'dog in the manger' spirit, and she would have been glad to get away from him, as she was fed up. Mabel was going to ask Mrs Evans if she realised her position.

. When the hearing was resumed on Thursday, 19th December, Casswell submitted that it was either an accident or murder, and he confidently suggested that it was not murder.

Addressing the jury, the Judge said they now knew something, but by no means all, as to what happened at East Appleford Farm. It seemed that relations between the prisoner and the dead man were anything but harmonious towards the date of the tragedy. Mrs Whittington, who seemed to be a very satisfactory witness and a person of sense and understanding, had said that the prisoner resented the dead man's association with Mrs Evans.

Mrs Whittington's evidence also corroborated the prisoner's story of the threats that the dead man had used.

Turning to the day of the tragedy, the Judge said: 'someone loaded this double-barrelled gun with one cartridge. I have heard no suggestion that the prisoner did this. Under those circumstances I think you are bound to deal with this aspect of the case on the footing that it is an accepted fact that it was the man who loaded it with one cartridge. If you start with that fact, you will probably ask why he loaded the gun with one cartridge. Whatever view you take of the prisoner's testimony, it is corroborated that there was a quarrel about this Mrs Evans, and you may think that this man did insert the cartridge, if not for the purpose of shooting the accused, at least for the purpose of threatening her. It seems to me a very material fact that he was the person who put the cartridge in the gun, and was in the first instance responsible for the tragedy that subsequently took place.'

The Judge then directed the jury that if they found the prisoner not guilty of murder, it would not be right for them to consider returning a verdict of manslaughter, as the prisoner's counsel had not had the opportunity to address them on the subject, which was not a charge made by the Crown.

After considering the case, the jury returned within ten minutes. They announced that had found Mabel Attrill not guilty.

Mabel burst into tears, and was still weeping bitterly when the Judge said, 'Let her be discharged'.

CHAPTER EIGHT

A SADISTIC MURDERER

Perhaps the most high-profile case in Casswell's distinguished career, certainly as far as the press and general public were concerned, was that of the defence of Neville George Heath some time after Mabel Attrill's trial, in 1946.

In June of that year the body of 32-year-old Margery Gardner was found in a room at the Pembridge Court Hotel in Notting Hill Gate. She had been badly mutilated and sexually assaulted. Her ankles were tied, her wrists had been bound and she had been suffocated. Her body bore the scars of seventeen whiplashes. The hotel room had been booked in the names of Lieutenant Colonel and Mrs Heath.

Two weeks later, posing as 'Group Captain Rupert Brooke', Heath met 21 year-old Doreen Marshall, who was taking a holiday alone at the Norfolk Hotel, Bournemouth. They met strolling on the promenade and he invited her for lunch at his hotel, the Tollard Royal. Having had lunch, he suggested that they should also dine together that evening at his hotel. This they did, and just before midnight he suggested seeing her back to her own hotel. It would appear that initially she refused, as she had asked for a taxi to be ordered. However, shortly afterwards Heath cancelled the taxi, saying that his guest would walk back to her hotel.

Doreen Marshall did not return to her hotel that night, and the following morning her absence was reported to the police and a search was begun. The following day, 5th July, the two hotel managers spoke with each other, as it was known that Doreen had taken a taxi from the Norfolk Hotel to the Tollard Royal on the evening of the 3rd July. Soon afterwards Mr Relf, the manager of the Tollard Royal, spoke to Heath and suggested that the missing lady was the one he had dined with. Heath laughed off Mr Relf's suggestion, saying his dining companion had been a lady he had known for years. However, shortly after this, Heath somewhat strangely telephoned the police station in Bournemouth, saying he might be able to help the police in this case. He rang again later, and was told that a photograph was now available of Doreen Marshall. Heath agreed to call in at the police station.

He arrived later that afternoon, and admitted that the photograph was that of the lady he had dined with. He told the detective constable that after they had left the Tollard Royal he had walked her back and left her at the entrance of the Norfolk Hotel. It was then that the police noticed his similarity to the man posing as Group Captain Brooke. The Metropolitan Police had circulated a photograph of Neville Heath to other Police Forces, saying he was wanted in connection with the murder of Margery Gardner.

The police already knew 29-year-old Heath, as he had a borstal record and had been tried by a court-martial for wearing uniforms and decorations he was not entitled to. In his jacket pocket was found a cloakroom ticket and the return half of a first-class rail ticket from Bournemouth to London. Subsequently the cloakroom ticket, issued from Bournemouth Station, was linked to a suitcase, which contained a bloodstained scarf and a metal-tipped whip. The rail ticket had been issued in the name of Doreen Marshall.

Heath was told he would be detained pending the arrival of officers from the Metropolitan Police. Later the police discovered that Heath had on the previous day pawned a ring and watch belonging to the missing Doreen. The next morning Heath was taken to London and charged with the murder of Margery Gardner.

On Monday 8th July the body of Doreen Marshall was found in Branksome Chine, concealed behind some rhododendron bushes. She was naked apart from the left shoe. She had been sexually assaulted and mutilated, and her throat had been cut. Her body had been covered by some of her clothing, which had been spread loosely on top of her. Some time afterwards Heath was charged with her murder.

On the 24th September 1946 the trial of Neville Heath for the murder of Margery Gardner began at the Old Bailey before Mr Justice Morris. The prosecution was led by Mr Anthony Hawke KC and the defence by Joshua Casswell KC.

Heath was charged with only one murder, that of Margery Gardner, because at the time only one murder could be included on the indictment. However Casswell deliberately brought in evidence about the second killing, in order to lay the foundations of the defence of insanity. Heath was not called to give evidence in the witness box, as Casswell was concerned that his calm and detached manner, together with his apparent intelligence, would not have convinced the jury that he was insane according to the McNaghten Rules. In order to establish a defence on the grounds of insanity, the defendant had to prove that he fell within the framework of the Rules, laid down over a hundred years before.

In 1842, a wood turner from Glasgow named Daniel McNaghten shot and killed Edward Drummond, private secretary to the then Prime Minister, Sir Robert Peel. He picked the wrong man, shooting Drummond by mistake instead of his intended target, the Prime Minister. At his trial it appeared that McNaghten was mentally unstable, but the question arose as to whether he could be held responsible for his actions due to his mental condition.

The Lord Chief Justice directed the jury that if McNaghten had been so carried away by his abnormal mental state as to have been incapable of knowing the difference between right and wrong, he should be found not guilty. Accordingly the jury acquitted him. As there was at that time no provision for a sending a convicted criminal to a mental institution such as Broadmoor, he was released. This caused much public concern, and consequently the House of Lords issued what were known as the McNaghten Rules.

Under these rules, to establish a defence on the grounds of insanity, it must be clearly proved that at the time of committing the act, the party accused was labouring under such a defect of reason, from disease of the mind, as not to know the nature and quality of the act he was doing, or, if he did know it, that he did not know that it was wrong. The burden of proof lay with the defendant, and there was to be the opinion of two psychiatrists 'on the balance of probability'.

In 1957 the Homicide Act introduced the defence of diminished responsibility, which stated that where a person kills or is party to the killing of another, he shall not be convicted of murder if he was suffering from such abnormality of mind (whether arising from a condition of arrested or retarded development of mind or any inherent causes or induced by disease or injury) as substantially impaired his mental responsibility for the acts or omissions in doing or being party to the killing.

Neville Heath was born in Ilford in 1917 and as a youth joined the Royal Air Force. However it was not long before he was sent to Borstal for three years for issuing dud cheques and other minor frauds. On his release, although having been court-martialled twice in this country, he joined the South African Air Force and rose to the rank of Captain, serving during the Second World War. In February 1942 he married Elizabeth, the daughter of a wealthy Johannesburg family. The marriage was not to last, and in spite of now having a son; Elizabeth divorced Heath for desertion in October 1945.

Very soon Heath faced his third court martial, for conduct prejudicial to good order and military discipline and for wearing military decorations to which he was not entitled. He was dismissed from the South African Air Force and returned to England in February 1946, where until his arrest he was studying for his commercial pilot's licence.

There was a great deal of public concern that after the discovery of Margery Gardener's body, the police had not released a photograph of Heath, their main suspect, to the public, so as it would be general knowledge what the suspect looked like. The press were obsessed with criticism of the police over this. In particular Doreen Marshall's father was adamant that had a photo been released, his daughter would probably still be alive. However, had this been done by the police any such disclosure could have rendered identification of Heath prejudiced by such publicity.

The prosecution called two expert witnesses, Dr H Grierson, Senior Medical Officer at Brixton Prison and Dr H Young, Senior Medical Officer at Wormwood Scrubs Prison. Both expressed the opinion that Heath was undoubtedly a sadist, a sexual pervert and possibly psychopathic, and that he had known what he was doing and knew it to be wrong. He was not suffering from any mental disease, and was not insane according to law.

After a three-day trial, the jury found Heath guilty and he was sentenced to death. Heath did not want to appeal his sentence, and Casswell doubted that had he done so, it would have been unlikely to succeed.

On the 26th October 1946, Neville George Cleverly Heath was hanged at Pentonville Prison. Apparently just before being led to the execution chamber he asked the Prison Governor for a whisky and followed this up by saying 'You might make that a double'.

In 1981 the television series *Lady Killers* screened an episode entitled *Make it a double*. The actor Paul Arlington played the part of Joshua Casswell.

CHAPTER NINE

THE FAILURE OF AN EXPERT WITNESS

✍

In 1951 Casswell left his legal practice and was appointed by the Lord Chancellor to the position of Official Referee, based in the Law Courts in the Strand. The Official Referee's Court was renamed in 1998, and is now known as the Technology and Construction Court. The range of cases tried in this court is considerable – mainly building and engineering disputes, but also including fire claims, sale of goods disputes and dilapidations cases. Casswell remained in this position until the end of 1958 on reaching the retirement age of seventy-two.

In 1961 he wrote his autobiography, entitled *A Lance for Liberty*. In his book Casswell revealed a disturbing fact concerning the Heath trial, in particular the use of an expert witness who turned out to be disastrous, especially for Heath. In order to establish that Heath was insane, Casswell would have to depend upon finding a top medical expert who would be prepared to say that at the time of Margery Gardner's killing, Heath did not know he was doing wrong. In due course he contacted Dr William Henry de Bargue Hubert, who had most impressive credentials. Having been psychiatrist to two hospitals, and formally psychotherapist at Wormwood Scrubs and Broadmoor, he was also joint author of a report, accepted by the Home Office as a standing authority, on psychological treatment in crime prevention – *The Psychological Treatment of Crime,* published in 1939.

After several interviews with Heath, Dr Hubert reported to Casswell: 'in my opinion this man ought to have been classified when young as a mental defective. He did not know he was doing wrong at the time of the murders'. To Casswell this provided a chance of establishing insanity under the McNaghten Rules, although Casswell's personal view was that Heath had probably committed both murders as a result of an irresistible, sexually inspired impulse to kill. However, in Dr Hubert he had an expert who was prepared to say that at the time of the offences Heath probably knew what he was doing, but was so mentally abnormal that he did not know that what he was doing was wrong.

Casswell could see that there could be holes in Dr Hubert's confident diagnosis, in particular the fact that Heath had tried to hide Doreen Marshall's body, which tended to indicate that he knew what he had done was wrong, together with the fact that he had robbed her of a ring and a watch which he later pawned, so this was not just sexual insanity. Therefore Casswell adopted the strategy of establishing *partial* insanity. This was an idea that had circulated in some academic circles, but at the time was not part of English law. It would be over ten years before the Homicide Act 1957 introduced 'diminished responsibility' as a possible defence. He could use the phrase *'partial insanity'* to convey to the jury that it was not inconsistent in their finding that the normally extremely self-possessed young man in the dock was also capable of the insane behaviour he had shown on two specific occasions when the normal restraints had suddenly given way.

However, when Dr Hubert was cross-examined by the prosecution, the chances of the jury finding Heath insane evaporated. The doctor allowed himself to be manoeuvred into a position where in the end he was saying in effect that Heath should be spared because he could not help himself. The prosecution had the doctor agreeing that a person who found it convenient to forge a cheque in order to free himself from financial responsibility was entitled to say that he thought it was right, and therefore was free from the responsibility of what he did. According to Casswell, and no doubt the jury, the expert witness for the defence was almost pleading for an indiscriminate licence to commit crime, because the criminal thinks his acts are right or necessary.

Casswell did his best on the re-examination of Dr Hubert, but the damage had already been done and it proved impossible to erase from the jury's mind the unfortunate impression his previous evidence must have given.

What Casswell did not know at the time, and was only to learn later, was that Dr Hubert was a drug addict. Within a few months of the trial Dr Hubert was dead. The coroner's verdict was 'death due to the combined effects of barbituric acid and chloral hydrate, self-administered'. Hubert died on the 5th March 1947, his 43rd birthday.

In his book Casswell says that on reading over the transcript he thinks he can detect a note of special pleading in Hubert's testimony, in that it would also serve to exonerate him from criminal responsibility for his own secret addiction. In seeking to excuse Neville Heath's conduct, he was endeavouring, albeit unconsciously, to excuse his own.

It will never be known whether the result would have been different if another expert been selected for the defence, or Hubert's evidence had not been so damaging. However it would have needed to be extremely forceful to counter the unequivocal opinions of the two doctors called by the prosecution. Albeit remote, there might have been sufficient doubt in the jury's mind that the outcome was a more favourable verdict, namely that Heath should be detained in Broadmoor at His Majesty's pleasure.

Joshua David Casswell died on the 15th December 1963. He was a truly remarkable man, not only a barrister who instigated a change in English law that saved numerous people from the gallows but a humanitarian who put justice before profit.

CHAPTER TEN

DECLINE AND FALL

There can be little doubt that Sir Bernard Spilsbury was a brilliant man, although it has been said of him that he was also arrogant and eccentric. He was able to communicate with the jury in a language that they understood and frequently his demeanour and reputation were sufficient for them to concur that his interpretation was the correct one and return a guilty decision. Of the nearly 200 murder trials in which he gave evidence for the prosecution, only a few ended in an acquittal.

A book published in 2007 entitled *Lethal Witness,* written by Andrew Rose QC, gives details of some of Spilsbury's cases in which the author concludes that the defendants were wrongly convicted of murder, based on what was essentially flawed evidence.

By the late 1930s Spilsbury's fame and flare was diminishing. He was already separated from his wife and personal tragedy was soon to strike. Shortly before the Mabel Attrill trial, his son Peter, also a doctor, was killed in the Blitz. Four years later another of his sons, Alan, died of tuberculosis. The losses of his sons must have been too much for him to bear. On the evening of the 17th December 1947, Spilsbury dined alone at his club. Afterwards he went to his laboratory in Gower Street at University College London. There he turned on a Bunsen burner tap and gassed himself to death.

In spite of his copious record keeping and his accumulation of forensic evidence on 4000 index cards during his lifetime (they are now publicly accessible at the Wellcome Library in London), Spilsbury left no note to explain his own death.

Sir Godfrey Baring, chairman of the Bench at Mabel Attrill's remand hearing, died in 1957 at the age of 86. During his life he held a remarkable record, being Chairman of the Isle of Wight Council for 51 years, from 1898 to 1949. A subsequent Chairman eloquently described why he had retained the post for so long: 'because the County Council thought that he was the best person to conduct their affairs'. He had also been an MP, the Island's High Sheriff, Deputy Lieutenant of Hampshire and an Alderman of London City Council. He also served as Chairman of the Royal National Lifeboat Institution for 33 years and in 1952, in recognition of his public service, he was awarded the title of Knight Commander, Order of the British Empire (KBE). He was so well known on the Island that even some school children respectfully referred to ball bearings as 'Godfreys'.

As for the fate of Dorothy O'Grady, the woman whose trial at Winchester Assizes had preceded that of Mabel Attrill's was something of an enigma. She was the only woman to be sentenced to death for spying in Britain during the Second World War. On appeal her sentence was commuted to 14 years' imprisonment, initially served at Holloway Prison, and latterly at Aylesbury Prison.

At the time little was known about her, because both her trial and the appeal were held in secret. She was born in 1897 in Clapham, London, and was known as Dorothy Pamela Squire. Before the trial she had been running a small boarding house in Sandown, living with her husband Vincent, a retired fireman with the London Fire Brigade. Vincent was absent from the family home for periods, as he had volunteered for fire-fighting duties during the Blitz. It has been argued that she was not a spy, but more of an amateur snoop and petty saboteur. Another writer, whose source cannot be substantiated, claimed that she was an Irish radical and was sending information to an address in Portugal.

Dorothy O'Grady came to the attention of the authorities in 1940 when she was seen on a regular basis walking her dog at the base of Culver Cliffs, just to the east of Sandown, which happened to be a prohibited area. This activity alerted the British Intelligence Service and her activities were monitored, including the interception of her mail. What exactly resulted from these covert observations is not known, but it was suggested that she visited sensitive locations on the Island and had been observed making sketches and taking notes. Eventually she was caught cutting a military telephone line and arrested for being in a prohibited area. She was granted bail while further enquiries were made. She then disappeared. There was concern that she might attempt to leave the Island, but she was eventually found living near Yarmouth under an assumed name. She was then charged under the Treachery Act and the Official Secrets Act and appeared at Winchester Assizes on the 16th December 1940.

It is unclear how Dorothy O'Grady, on being released from prison, spent the rest of her life, except that she returned to the Island, eventually living at Porter Close, Flitcroft Gardens, Lake. She died in 1985, at the age of 87. The truth and motivation of her wartime activities may ever remain a mystery.

The Isle of Wight History Centre reported that they assumed much more would be revealed when her file was declassified. They state that the file was finally released at The National Archives in January 2006. However, on the 23rd February the Home Office recalled the file from The Archives 'in the conduct of official business'. Six months later, when the National Archives requested return of the file, the Home Office said it could no longer be traced. Therefore it seems unlikely that any member of the public got to see the documents in the brief period they were available. A Freedom of Information request has been lodged with the Home Office to try and retrieve any internal memoranda referring to the files, but it is not expected to reveal much.

So due to either carelessness or negligence, or - in the opinion of some - for a more sinister reason, the full story of the 'Sandown Spy' may remain an enigma.

However in June 2012 a new book appeared, written by author and journalist Adrian Searle. *The Spy Beside the Sea* was written with the benefit of previously classified material and examines the story and background of Dorothy O'Grady, together with her possible motives.

What eventually happened to Reginald Woolmington is also unclear. A man who in 1935 held a unique position in English Law faded away, if not into obscurity, certainly out of the public eye. What is known is that on the eve of his release, having been held in the condemned cell in Pentonville Prison for nearly three months, and only three days before he was due to be hanged, he gave an interview to the *Daily Express*. He said that during the whole time he had been in custody he had been healthy and had a certain peace of mind. The only time he had been shaken had been when he heard his death sentence back in February at Bristol Assizes. When the terrible thought hit him that his wife Violet whom he loved, was dead and that he was to be hanged, he broke down for a while. However the thought that he was not a murderer, and had not in fact harmed any man or woman in his life, had given him some comfort. An additional source of solace was that every night the prison chaplain had come to talk with him and they had prayed together. Before this he said that he had not been very religious.

Woolmington went on to say that he had been in love with Violet for two and a half years, since she was fifteen. He had first met her when she had walked across the field while he was haymaking with his father. He had in fact returned from Jersey, where he had been working, the previous summer to marry her.

His young son, who had been only two months old when he had last seen him, was being brought up in a home in Kensington. Woolmington thought he would not be allowed to see him, but he decided to try, as the child was the only thing in the world he could call his own. He intended to spend a few months at home and then go away from England, probably to Jersey for the next potato season. When that was over, he would get another job and stay there for good.

He said that the only thing he could never forget about the past few months was the way he was defended and given legal aid, although he was practically penniless. All he had now was five shillings and the clothes he stood up in. He continued by saying that it was wonderful to think that a farm labourer with no money could get to the House of Lords, the highest court in Britain, to find justice. Only a couple of hours before he had been standing between two warders as Prisoner number 3454; now he was Reginald Woolmington again, farm labourer and free man.

Several weeks later, Joshua Casswell received a letter from Woolmington thanking him for all his help and asking for some advice. He had been offered a well-paid turn at a music hall, employment as a gardener or the chance of starting a new life in South Africa. Casswell thought that as he had no qualifications as an entertainer, and his music hall career would no doubt have lasted only as long as the public remained interested in the case, he advised Woolmington to start a new life in South Africa.

The next and only time Casswell heard from Woolmington again, he learned that he had started a good job, given by a well-wisher, but had left soon afterwards. Perhaps his past experiences and notoriety had been too much and too soon for him to be able to settle down.

EPILOGUE

After the war Mabel Attrill was living in Sandown, and on St Valentine's Day 1948 she married Albert, a widower, and moved into his house in Alvington Road, Carisbrooke. There would appear to have been no animosity between Mabel and Frank Cave's daughter, as Doris Whittington was a witness at the Register Office. Two years later Mabel and Albert had a son. However, misfortune was to strike when in 1952 Albert sadly died, just 61 years old.

In 1967, Mabel now aged 52, remarried. Her new husband, Charles Cooper, also a widower, was employed as a psychiatric nurse at the local hospital. He and Mabel lived together in Carisbrooke for nearly 40 years. Mabel died in 2005, days short of her ninetieth birthday.

Today, more than 70 years after the case, questions still remain. Why at the scene of the shooting was the hammer over the left barrel of the shotgun found in the cocked position? This was a question that was not addressed during the investigation or at Mabel's trial. According to the evidence of PC Sampson, the first policeman at the scene, he saw the shotgun in the corner of the porch and found an empty cartridge case in the right barrel, and as would be expected the hammer was in the down position. He also found that the left barrel did not contain a cartridge but that the hammer was in the cocked position. Older shotguns of that type did not have a safety catch as such, so the hammer would first be cocked, enabling the trigger to be pulled, the hammer released and hitting the percussion cap in the cartridge and firing the gun.

Frank was obviously experienced in the use of his gun, so after loading the right barrel, unless he was intending to fire it immediately, why had he cocked the right hammer? More strangely perhaps, why cock the left hammer over an empty barrel?

Perhaps a more likely explanation was that after loading the gun Frank had not cocked either hammer. So did both hammers become cocked during his struggle with Mabel? We are unlikely ever to know the full story of what happened that day.